The Way We Came

Other books by the author

Poetry
Dandelions for Mothers' Day (Stride 1988 and 1989)
The Fiddle: New and Selected Poems (Stride 1999)

The Least Thing (Editor, Stride 1989)
Making Connections: A Festschrift for Matt Simpson (Editor, Stride 1996)

The Way We Came

Angela Topping

Published by bluechrome publishing 2007

2 4 6 8 10 9 7 5 3 1

Copyright © Angela Topping 2007

Angela Topping has asserted her right under the Copyright,
Designs and Patents Act 1988 to be identified as the author
of this work

First published in Great Britain in 2007 by
bluechrome publishing
PO Box 109,
Portishead, Bristol. BS20 7ZJ

www.bluechrome.co.uk

A CIP catalogue record for this book is available from the
British Library

ISBN 978-1-904781-44-8

Contents

"Even such is Time that takes in trust
Our youth and joy, our all we have,
And pays us but with earth and dust."

Sir Walter Raleigh

"What see'st thou else
In the dark backward and abysm of time?"

Shakespeare: The Tempest

"O! Call back yesterday, bid time return."

Shakespeare: Richard II

"…the best word that I wanted to say to you
is the word that I have not yet said."

Nasim Hiknet translated by Richard McKane

"We are not free. And the sky can still fall on our heads."

Antonin Artaud

Acknowledgements

Books:

Making Connections (Stride 1996)
Voices for Kosovo (Stride 1999)
The Way you Say the World (Shoestring 2003)
Sounding Heaven and Earth (The Canterbury Press and The Spire Trust 2004)
Life Lines (Poems from the High Sheriff's Prize for Literature; Chester Academic Press 2005)

Magazines:

Brando's Hat; nthposition; Orbis; Other Poetry; Prop; Slop; Stride; The Affectionate Punch; The Reader.

Special thanks are due to Matt Simpson, sternest critic and dear friend.

Cover photograph of Stickle Tarn, The Lake District, by Gordon Tyrrall.

Translate This

(*For Anne Stevenson*)

All language is the translation of hungers into sounds
                                        Michele Roberts

Language lies on the tongue.
Its babble rises from hungers
in the dark; in a need for answers;
in black water, stiff with ice.

Fire, food, warmth, water - words
of people finding sounds can signify.
Rhythms of words beaten out
in dancing feet or echoing drums,
words - the first ordering of sense.

I see is amazement,
No is power, and calling for things
brings them magically to hand. Words
too few to lie. Feel them in your mouth,
come to know their texture after the tongue
tires of rattles and spoons of slop.

Signs on the page that can speak
in the private mind mean stories
whenever they are wanted,
soothing a whining child to silence,
make a world to crawl inside, to travel time
and spin the galaxy like a roundabout.

Language on the page whispers 'I'm here',
when the writer's formless dust.
Take Catullus' hendecasyllables -
insinuating hate, sharp insults centuries old,
to fit live tongues though his is dead.

From dead empires disseminated words
infect the air. In libraries
words sleep, waiting for readers' eyes
to wake them with a glance. Listen,
as soon as books open, voices command,
babbling of hungers lying in the dark.

Sea Change

What the sea does, and does so well,
is to embrace and change
all things to its cool element.

From the *Titanic* a suitcase is lifted,
like a drowned dog, its body leaking;
folded, laundered shirts are stained.

A pile of crumbling junk, that ship;
crunching bacteria fasten
nibbling mouths on its very steel;

the railings' fur of barnacles
outlives the stoles of women.
The champagne may still be drinkable.

On the ocean floor in pliés
pairs of boots point outward toes.
Rusticles hang like crystallised tears.

Shoals of fish play small chase
in and out the rusty portholes.
Where is Hartley's violin?

Taffeta

Take me to the ocean, I said.
I wore my ocean-green shot taffeta skirt.
The wind shifted its colours
from red to green, making it
a magic lantern, glittering
like the opalescent sea.
The dunes stretched for miles.
Cars shimmered in the heat haze
like jewels. Released from austerity -
an exam room weighted with words -
I wanted to see space, a wide horizon,
sky full of gulls, gossiping.
I wanted to be lapped by a salt tide,
buffeted by waves and cleansing winds.
My white legs became a mermaid's tail,
my toes sensed the ribbed sand,
imprinted by travelling waves.
You took me home from the ocean
that summer and married me.

Dialectic

The love of angels is pure and lofty.
You dine on clouds, eat with silver spoons
and in ice palaces, honeymoon.
You fly in a flurry of white wings,
roost in trees for fun and frighten poets.
The kiss of an angel is like drinking champagne.
When you enter a room, lights blaze
to a fanfare of trumpets and caviar.

The love of devils is all beating hearts, drums
and the thrum of insane lust.
He touches you, leaving a burnt paw-print,
a love bite. He brings you gifts of brimstone
for your bath, his halo made of steam.
His eyes burn with desire when he makes you
Java Lava coffee, offers Turkish Delight.
He cannot marry you. None of this is real.

Morning

Lifting a lid off the world,
the first fingers of light
intrude upon the sky.
The faint sun is spying,
banishing distant stars,
undoing the pins of night.

Crickets wake to creak
their greeting to the day –
another night survived.
Slugs refill their silver tracks.
Small birds compete
in raucous noise.
Pink worms wriggle in their soil.

You should have been there
holding my hand:
Adam and Eve at the gates of Eden,
taking one last look.

Menai Morning

Dawn rises slowly over the Straits;
a creeping light slips through mist.
The pines observe like sage old men
who have seen it all thousands of times.
Across the water the mountains
keep fast their secrets. I would
bring you a morning such as this
for walking through woods, our skin
turning from blue to ivory as broad day
replaces the shreds of night.

Salt

I love you as fresh meat loves salt

There is a kind of love that wants for nothing
merely time to wade deep in the salt waters
of eyes so wise they need no words to say.

There is a kind of love that arises smiling
from separate beds in separate towns
rejoicing in the existence of the other.

This love needs no promises, no ceremonies
its every shared meal is a dedication,
every seasoned memory an affirmation.

Iona

I came too late
at the appointed time
a chapel on a windy hill
to meet your echo
blue peace and yearning sky
I reach for you
Celtic crosses, seaworn stone
aching places of our hearts
shore of silver sand
music is the only language
wombsound and cradle song
the day unravels
seasound and grave song
codes and uncodes suspend time
words rise up as though pressed from hidden places
time does not do this on purpose

First House

As the key fits the lock
with smug knowledge,
and the kettle shuts off,
presenting its steam
to the chill morning,
your colour and order
will inhabit this house.

Around you walls
narrate your histories,
as piece by piece of you
is carried here.
You welcome me as one
who is accepted,
a guest of your hearth.

Going Back in Time

Speke Hall, Liverpool

Aeroplanes agitate the air, crumple the sky
for one noisy moment, then time settles back.
A troupe of nineteen-sixties schoolgirls,
crocodiled by pencil-skirted Miss
crosses the bridge of stone
stiffened by reminders of school rules.

*

William Morris wallpaper is carefully smoothed,
the servants wonder at new electric lights,
new-fangled stuff in the kitchen. A roundhead
thunders over the bridge across the moat.
Father James tucks himself
into the secret cell to pray while white
Tudor faces peer from mullioned windows.

*

Adam and Eve live from wedding anniversary
to wedding anniversary; their ancient branches
a citadel, their new leaves gossiping
in spring wind as a cobbled courtyard is hammered
into place around their roots. Exiled from the garden,
seedling strength matching inch by inch,
they watch the new house rise with them.

Note: Adam and Eve are the names of a pair of ancient yew trees in the inner courtyard. They pre-date any house on the site.

Madingly Hall, Cambridge

for Matt Simpson

So this is where you fished at night,
carp clooping in the lake, worm dipped
in lush waters, while Up North,
I was relinquishing amniotic dreams.
Your working-class earnestness poked into books
heavy with privilege and class, the yokel
poaching the estate, filching the necessary
from careless plenty. *My Cambridge*
you write in a poem that howls with loss.

II

My turn for earnest studentship. You, college lecturer,
pointed out as *poet*. I tendered poems
for judgement and was redeemed: one image,
you said, *had something*.

III

After ten years severance I write a letter
to your old address, approaching your presence
in my life again as if returning to a state of grace,
a listening out for sounds from another life.
Your reply to *my once, my erstwhile student*
rushed back. Your writing hadn't changed.
We re-encountered each other - finding echoes
in half lines: your heart attack, my labours.
Again I became your student,
nudging scared poems across a library room
under hostile gaze, from which you would defend me,
yet send me home sometimes in tears from one hard look
nothing to do with criticism.

IV

Dedicated to you, I have arrived in book form.
have learned my lessons well,
a model pupil who can astonish you
sometimes in a half line. Here are poems
you have teased me into getting right,
grown up and going out on their first date.

V

Here, at Madingley,
I am studying poetry with someone else
but address my thoughts to you in Liverpool.
In topiary gloom, my back against an oak,
I pause to sing a ballad of love against all odds.
Walking in the Knot garden, I meet your ghost.
You pace, patient with me, we stroll and talk.
We would not be sad together here, nor would you
lead me like a dumb animal. Our animus
is always to be content together, bubbling with
(there does not seem another word) love.
Had I been here with you, *what larks, Pip?*
Or *how all occasions do conspire ... !*

VI

I have longed to be your exact contemporary,
to share your *Goon Show* lingo, to have known
your childhood war, to have tasted danger
like rationed sweets fizzing on the tongue.

You write *And then Angela* of a not-me
too fond of shopping and duff music
but say you *truly loved* her and it hurts,
even with the tongue in the cheek.
I talk of tongues: not just the strawberry-flesh
of forbidden mouths, but words, words, words,
the matter of friendship, always.

First Song

One thing they can never do
is wake together in one bed,
drink fresh coffee, taken black,
in a sunlight-dazzled room. Nor can
they share a joyful hour, playing songs,
sip nettle wine; no trying out
guitar tricks; cooking up exotic feasts.
None of that.

And so, what's left for those
who messed up all their chances? The sun
still pinkly climbs the sky, the coffee beans
release their aroma, words of songs
have resonance for them alone;
and instead of pillow talk, electronic mail.

Love is... Finally this

So Adrian Henri's gone. Affable host of Liverpool 1;
iconographer of Canning Street; genial soul of every bar
dispensing compliments and beer. What's love now?

Haunt your old haunts, Adrian. That huge cathedral's too grand.
You're more the poet of chippies, back street pubs, backs of vans.
Your eyes-closed readings betrayed the shy lack of faith in self.

I hope there's a heaven made for you, of scotch in the afternoons,
the stained-glass colours of your paintings and a procession
of dolly-bird angels for you to eye like the Everlasting Sixties.

Emily's Garden

The Old Parsonage, Haworth

There's a tumbledown washhouse
nibbled by ivy. Nettles and dandelions,
the ingredients of pop, skulk in the corner.
Linen is on the line, crisply pegged.
The only blooms here are wild.
Ragged robin, herb robert and purple loosestrife
flourish with neglect. The vegetable plot
requires her nurture. She hoes there,
excising weeds from potatoes,
beans, exotic carrots, comfortable swede.
Granite rocks are the vertebrae of her soil.
She pushes dark hair behind her ears,
toils away at daily tasks. The bread
will only rise for her, the heel of her hand
shows it who's mistress. But at night
by tallow, in unsmiling joy, she writes.

A Room for William

Visit to Dove Cottage

Somewhere he won't be disturbed.
Kitchen questions drown out the emotion
he needs *tranquillity* to *recollect.*
His elegant chair was made for
a gentleman wearing a sword.

Downstairs, his wife shushes the children.
Upstairs William commands the view:
ringed fells and reedy mere. This patchwork
was pieced by Dorothy. Like wise, the rag rug.
She has the skill of using up the scraps.

From her morning walk she brings
the post, three letters from friends,
then tiptoes away. Let us leave William
with his books, pictures
and yet unread letters.
A poem may be hatching.
Hush, children, don't you bother him.

Miranda to Ferdinand

For a whole year we played chess.
I arranged my room for you, setting up
the chessboard's gleaming ranks until
each pawn was standing to attention.
I castled my king to keep him snug,
but you always broke through effortlessly.
Without a second thought,
you ravished my queen, left me defenceless.
Your knights galloped over my fields, trampling
my pieces. I always surrendered,
you refused to claim your spoils.
I was there for the taking. What more
could any woman have done? Checkmate.

Fool

Jab Jab,
rattling bells,
never letting up.

He quips, mangles words
until they're marmalised,
hardly know themselves.

Harlequin, chequerboard his clothes,
three-horned hat, pointed boots,
smile-curling toes.

Taut on high wire,
spying out secrets,
he's in the know.

Sees right through
opalescence, taffeta minds -
unfooled by disguise,

knows the right song -
the one that tells you
all you need to know.

His name is legion :
Feste, Touchstone, loonface,
Poor Tom, clown.

Four Curiosities

The Burrell Collection, Glasgow

i Shawabtis for a Teacher
Small figure buried with the dead Egyptian to do his work in the underworld

Oh Shawabtis, take my class,
detail for me the forced labour
of making them listen.
Flood their banks with knowledge,
cultivate their poor unyielding fields
with the good thought, marching
ideas towards unconquered heads.
Oh Shawabtis, mark their work,
lift up my pen and track mistakes,
carry books east and west, you whose job it is
to stand for me in the underworld.

ii The Expectancy Glass

Glass used by a lady to announce her pregnancy

May the launch of the little ship proceed well (1790)

I'm sure I saw Charlotte drink
from the expectancy glass.
Did you see? *They say truth*
comes peeping
over the rim of the glass
when dinner's done.
With a secretive smile
she sipped her cordial,
the inscription towards her.

I'm sure I saw Charlotte smile.
What do you think
so soon after the last?
Will we see Charlotte
in full sail again? She was
always too soft-hearted
for her own good.

iii The Casket

There's a grammar of stitches to learn,
to prick onto this coarse linen
while brothers learn Latin and Greek,
copy them to parchment.

This casket is my work of accomplishment.
It's to hold jewels and spices
when I am wife, like Susannah,
whose story I chose to sew.

I must be stitch perfect or mother
will make me unpick again.
My alphabet of cotton
is all I have
to conquer the world.

iv Misericords

Mischievous hands carved
these cartoons in oak -
twitching mice on ears of wheat,
grimacing goblins -
for monks to rest on,
some relief
from being upright
in icy chapel
intoning plainsong
before the day claims them
as men who toil.

Seconds Out on Saturdays

Saturday afternoons:
the alien atmosphere
of wrestling on the telly.

No speech or mithering.
Just watch as one fat man
slams another down.

A pugilistic referee shouts
Seconds out. Worse
than playground fights.

Grown men, slathered with
sweat, grunt while my father,
brothers, egg them on.

And Mother in the kitchen,
presiding over suds,
wrestles with sheets.

Father's Bronchitis

I listen for
the creak of panic in his lungs
as he leans on pedals to confront
a hill.

I know his days on bikes are slowing,
the cycle chain ticks off the miles.
Trees and fields and lanes slip by.
And years.

I clutch my sheaf of flowers tight
knowing the house will stifle them.
He sits by open kitchen door,
for air,

gasping like a landed carp.
There's nothing I can do except
brew up the way he likes, put away
the bike.

Father, Gardening

He is nowhere now
so I can place him here,
leaning on a rake
plotting colour schemes,
knowing our garden's best.

He moves into the greenhouse
to cup the warm weight
of tomatoes in his hand.
Each plant is knotted,
rigged with twine and cane
in terracotta pot, like a galleon
earthed in its bottle.

There's nowt like Ailsa Craig,
he'd say, whispered name
mingling with green incense,
the intimate spice of tomatoes
and my father telling secrets.

Better there than in the ruined garden,
his greenhouse shattered and glassless.
Mowing lawns left him *out of puff,*
defeated. He'd stare through the window
at stacked terracotta pots,
some cracked with frost, watching –
in rain he dare not go out in –
red peonies smash to the ground.

Second Best

She'd never wanted to outlive his care,
his dogged strength, his cups of tea at nine,
gas fire and telly on, his firm hand holding hers.

She wept within my arms, light as a child.
I never thought he'd let me down like this
while upstairs elder brother knelt beside
the bed where our dead father lay. Less than
an hour before, I'd wished my dad good night,
a better sleep than his last, troubled one.

Two years later, straight from work, I ran
to join the ward's impatient queue.
Your dad was first in every night, she said.

Broken Tokens

In their padded, bought-in box I keep
what still remains of diamonds and of gold.
Too good to last, too pure to wear, the rings
he bought her first, now sliver thin and old.

What should I do with broken tokens now?
He hasn't gone to sea, and she can't wait
his safe return on shore. And this cooled gold
is trinket that can never be remade.

Players Navy Cut

My father, asthmatic, always smoked.
At seventeen he was sophisticate, biting on a pipe,
impressing my gauche mother with his film-star looks.

Players Navy Cut was the brand of fags he liked.
I loved the cherry smell that clung
to folded silver paper begged from boxes

but hated the stains made by a lit cigarette
burning on the side of the bath while he spent
hours locked in there reading the paper.

Hated his smoking, as mother had grown to,
once we realised he was killing himself slowly.
He liked saving up his vouchers; it seemed

the more he smoked, the more he could
write away for, in his well-tutored copperplate.
The picture of a salty sailor on the packet,

head wreathed by tarry rope, had come to be
my father as he might have been if his father
had let him join the navy at eighteen.

Smoking was his way of being carefree,
the sailor he might have become,
white-bearded, weathered, venerable.

Frankincense

Smoking is something I've always hated:
its paraphernalia of dog ends, lighters, ash.
I worry for your lungs and arteries.

Yet when you strike a match and pull
gratefully on the pale insidious stalk
in the quiet companionship of my back doorstep,

the thready rising wisp of smoke
carried off into the scented evening
is flame of sanctuary lamp,

mysterious as the Holy Spirit,
red-eye presence in the night church,
blue as frankincense.

This Time

I

This time of year I get to thinking
and you not here to talk to of my thoughts.
I think of you in Spain, watching days vanish
as cycle wheels clock up the miles.
I think about the times you arrive
empty-handed on my doorstep, bringing
so much and so much, too much sometimes
for me to take hold of and not drop.
The weather is dazzling and the evening sky
pink as a kiss.

II

We meet on a rainy afternoon. It is time
for one of my lessons. You are teaching me
contentment. We watch the afternoon drift
indifferently downriver, passing as time must.
We look at things without a need to possess –
by your quiet waters there is nothing I shall want.

To Narnia and Back

Church Stretton

A trip for the day: giddy as kids, we find
a fold in time - Thirties shop fronts, bunting
threading streets as if to welcome us,
though we travel incognito. Both
of us still half-believe in magic, share
a common childhood time of being wise.

We talk of childhood books and wild beliefs-
your love of Shropshire since the days you read
adventure books set in its secret hills;
my camels stalk those hills as when at five
my father pointed out their lumpen backs.
I recognise in you the boy you were.

Walking on Long Mynd, through furze and ling,
we seek out separate landmarks from the past.
I tell of Tam Lin, snatched by faeries; you try
to scare the sheep. We follow-my-leader,
know that magic is in people too.
Why can't time fold back upon itself,
concertina to make each choice a life?

Inhabiting this tuck in time, we pass
an iron lamp post straight from Narnia,
in always summer grow old here
in that cottage with diamond panes;
going back with both our lives intact,
tumbling back through a wardrobe
to lives that have a claim on us.

Time Piece

It wears whatever face it can.
No longer wound or put right.
Whichever way you turn, it's owl.
Round socket eyes fit a fingertip.
My fingers stir seconds long
ticked away, the minute cogs
keep precisely their appointed track.
Once they regulated lives,
were consulted about trains, arrivals,
banished all hope of lovers' promises
ever being kept. Now its jewels
are useless trash, its silver surface
marred, its rivets unriveting, loose.
A day, a week, a life, is held
in my shut hand, as light as bone.

Calling me on the Phone

was an ordeal then:
you, pathologically shy,
no phone anyway,
a long walk to the nearest call box.

Me, shy too,
hating answering the thing
that squatted blackly
in the garishly-papered hall.

Yet we had our first big row
on the telephone,
you, full of beer and justified wrongs,
angry that I had failed to show.

Me, staying in, tearful,
waiting for a summons
that never came. Rebellious,
I slammed down the phone.

Oh, we patched it up
after a fashion, but both know
these things happen,
if not one way then another.

Can't blame the telephone,
can't blame each other.

Happy Birthday, Mr President

for Marilyn Monroe

Madison Square Gardens had never seen a mermaid.
Now, here she was, so far from home she'd never go back.
Stitched into the dress, a cage around her flesh, so tight
there's no mannequin in all America could fit in.

Served up in sheer silk, studded
with the weight of six thousand diamante stones,
a gauzy tail. More enticing than naked, she looked,
as she sang and blew her angel's kiss to *Mr President.*

One spark could have ignited her where she stood,
the dress a confection of flammable fabric.
No-one cared that night as they stitched her in
each pin-tight tack holding her fast. *Happy Birthday.*

Old Selves

Open a cupboard in your head
in that book-lined junk-filled room
cluttered with the narratives you invent
for your own life. Be brave, clasp the brass
key and unwind. What do you find?
This is where you keep your childhood terrors
in a box with a rusted lock. Don't look.
Your long dead loves are here, glowing
in the distant dark. All the things you've lost –
a doll with a broken face, the skeleton
of a seahorse, fragile with age – tumble out,
sift through your fingers, leaving stains.
Your old selves live here, still breathing softly.

The Attic

To enter the attic is to be lost.
Up the ladder into the too warm
fly-trapping darkness beneath the eaves
to find an old dressing up frock
or Christmas presents carefully hidden
over the sleeping heads of the children.

Boxes full of secrets and memories,
things we can't bear to discard.
Open a box and baby cardigans
stained from mixed feeding
appeal to be used again. Old letters
unfold themselves in remembering hands.

Passing It On

I weigh out exact divisions
of flour and fat, mix with milk
as grandma, sixty years dead, used to do.
You both insist on dragging chairs
to halt each elbow, supervise
as I roll out on floured board.

You lean to swipe strips of dough,
pestering with questions while I
pinch and trim and tailor
pastry to plates. Parallel lines
slit the centre to let out steam.
With flourish of brush and knife
I cut and glue veined leaves of dough.

For loss of swiftness I've traded
continuity. *My mother did it this way*
you'll both say to hampering audiences
as you mix with milk and deftly press your knives.

Searching for Snow

Press your nose against the pane,
wish for it. Scan the sky. Listen
for the silence of every living thing
braced against the cold.

You want snowmen, snowball contests,
to be snowed in, kept off school.

Some hope, except in dreams
of dragging caked mittens from tingling fingers,
sipping hot chocolate, regressing to *Watch with Mother*.

Snow remakes the world for however long it lasts
until the tension goes out of it. As childish
as innocence before grown-up boots stamp it out.

Closure

Year 11 Leavers' Prom

Tonight I'm letting my hair down. A teacher
not much longer, I groove with the kids;
roll on the floor in rows; conga round the garden,
take smoking lessons. Fail.

These students understand:
they've suffered Leaver Fever too,
know how it feels.

I've spent the last six years crucifying their mistakes
with crosses along the Appian Way, erasing myself
from blackboards each day. Now
I'm clearing out, unpinning displays.

Words are my stock in trade. I want
to give them away. But now
I have run out of words to say.

Mastering the Guitar

The mysteries of tablature yield
shape by shape. The strings sing their metal
sentences. None of this is enough.

*

In Clarksdale once, a man
sold his soul for mastery,
to be King of the Blues.
He found a totem place, crossroads.

Take the bone from a cat, black
as a shellacked guitar, black
as the skin of Robert Johnson himself,
the devil's slave now. Unwrap your guitar.

Start to play the only way you can.
Keep pickin'. Sense another's breathing.
Hear the pluck of unseen hands,
press your fingers without cease,

frets stain with blood
blue as the Blues in the ghostly dark.
Let the whites of your eyes show
white as bone, in full moon light,

playing your immortal soul away.
You're branded now, master.
You can play any tune, embellish
and syncopate like the devil himself.

Go home in morning silence
and astonish your friends. It will be enough.
Any tune you like, remember.

*

Travellers to Clarksdale, where
Highway 61 and Highway 49
cross one another in the night,
find only a bricked-up Laundromat.

Squatters' rights, on Johnson's corner,
lye soap to wash away the blues.
Too many poor folk here, the devil's
long moved on.

Forfeit

Time tricks memory : it's in the senses.
A flash of sunlight on brick and suddenly
clear as film you see a road walked down once
thirty years ago, hear the voice of someone long dead.

A smell can do it too. The patina of the library
polish overlaid with dust, smell careering out
with the first swing of the revolving door, like an embrace
pulling you in to time trapped between plastic coated covers.

Inside you feel the same. You're not.
You're onion, pass-the-parcel prize without
inside, hollow and afraid. You're all forfeit.

Time Travel

You can practise this technique at home :
make still the air as birds in wintertime,
select a half-forgotten song to play,
set a flame to one white candle,
softly, softly close the curtained eyes.
From memory the streets will re-appear.
You will know how to find your way on pavements
of tarmac, tacky from an afternoon of sun.
Step backwards into time. Cut to a room -
the bed is rainbow-spread, the room is stuffed
with shells and chessmen, books, one blue guitar.
Speak to the inmate dreaming on the pillow -
you will not need to ask her name.

Such Trust

Deep in all the years that tried to sever us
some raw crystals remain bedded down in rock.

Not least that time in the back of my sister's beat-up mini
in the darkness of a lift back from the pub

as I was nestling on your bony shoulder, you dropped your guard
a few silent seconds to rest your head on top of mine:

the warm weight of it, that small gesture of trust
a momentary relaxation of shyness.

Playing

for Fergus

Cast as the lovers in *Blood Wedding*,
over the script we eye each other.
We have to believe the fiction.

Our scene is sensual, symbolic.
We are both afraid. Your hair's
tied back, straight, thick, dark.

I am teacher, unbreakable.
Yet you lift me down from a chair
as if lifting a plate from a shelf.

We have to acquire a history.
You take off your hat. We find
velvet and satin to clothe our new selves.

Shy, we utter Lorca's lines, then
throw away the script. We have
run away together to this wood.

If they separate us we will be dead.
We have to learn trespass. Look
at me when you say *I love you.*

Palm to palm with outstretched arms
my head at your heart – this the embrace
we devise and hold. Stillness.

At the day's end, our lives as lovers end.
You embrace me freely, kiss my face.
Darkness falls between us, an honourable sword.

Charged

Rain clings to pavements.
Inside people stand haloed
by steam and light. Sinuously
I wind through crowds
to find friends' backs to me.

Kisses pop on my hot cheek
each one a licked finger testing
a heated iron. The mettle of me
hissing and heavy in the café's
glass box of light.

The heat of other kisses
smoothed on linen faces
soothes and comforts.
Leaving, I press your lips
lightly with mine.

No danger. The circuit's
earthed. Under this roof
there are no stars to steer by,
throw us off course. Time,
as ever, is implacable.

Anus

Sweetly puckered-up pink mouth
uttering words only comprehensible
to the nose. Bubbly syllables
rising effortlessly, the babble of gastronomy.
A language only permitted
between intimates, who answer to
your repertoire of sound and fruity odours.
This is warm, with no false airs, like a sloppy kiss.

The Butcher's Shop

The pigs are strung in rows, open-mouthed,
dignified in martyrs' deaths. They hang
stiff as Sunday manners, their porky heads
voting Tory all their lives, their blue rosettes
discarded now. The butcher smiles a meaty smile,
white apron stained with who knows what,
fingers fat as sausages. Smug, woolly cattle
and snowy sheep prance on tiles, grazing
on eternity, cute illustrations in a children's book.
What does the sheep say now?
Tacky sawdust clogs your shoes.
Little plastic hedges divide the trays of meat,
playing farms. All the way home
your cold and soggy paper parcel bleeds.

Officium Defunctorum

Liverpool Metropolitan Cathedral
Music by Hilliard Ensemble and Jan Garbarek, Saxophonist

With muffled feet around the marbled floor
the cantors stalk to tantalise our ears.
We sit and shiver in the spectral chill.
A saxophone cuts in to tell our fears.
Across their lullaby of chants in praise
of God and his great mercy unto us
the saxophone inserts a swastika
and one by one the faces of the lost
appeal to our mercy, long denied;
the homeless, loveless, smelly, dangerous, mad,
the not-quite Christ. Just now in the pub
we shrugged away a stranger and were glad.
Outside the air is frost-infested, chill,
and lips that used to pray are dumb and still.

Nights in the Old City

There's something dying in this place tonight.
It wrestles with the dark but cannot last.
The streets are wet and comfortless.

There's plenty of time for talking as we sit,
coffee cooling past its power to soothe.
Your naked glance, despairing, catches me
off guard; I am unable to perform
my usual magic trick of raising smiles.

You measure time in cigarettes while I
sip cognac, try to thaw your mood.
We risk a walk despite the rain and find
a draughty church; with votive candles lit,
we watch the shadows flutter crazily,
talk of old inevitable things.

The Way We Came

I found you over the horizon.
I was looking the other way,
backwards across the valley,
the Cheshire plain in darkness.

Wires in the dark –
we still connect after all this time.

When I look at you I want
to save you from the lines on your face.

Your white-knuckled hands,
nails still slightly bitten
are strange and familiar.
The little moons of your glasses
and your half-closed grey-green eyes
petition me wordlessly.

What is to be done?
The backlit angel in the churchyard
knows nothing, her back turned away
from our two blind faces
as we stumble on, blundering,
bewildered, into the present.

Who can direct us back the way we came?

Arrival

It's the smells that whisper home.
You cling to them for calm.
Aroma of fresh coffee rises
through cottage floorboards
like incense, when you wake
in unfamiliar sheets. There's a
tang of aspen buds,
earth's April musk.

Soft light of white-walled villages
enters your head. Hollyhocks,
delphiniums embroidered on houses.
Lamps are lit but not for you.
Far from home, the rainy glass
divides you from the landscape.
You're a bug, amber-stopped.
Remember, you have chosen this.

The country that you travel through
is spiritual mountains,
hiero and glyph, myths,
other people's loves, forays into
deserts, shorelines, wine-strong streets.
You're pulled along, surrendered
to tracked predestinations.
The only thing you can do is arrive.

Facing Up To It

Oh but to die and leave this sensible warm motion
Measure for Measure

The knowledge that one day I will
be called to leave behind all this
that I have loved: my books
both read and yet to read; my music,
and handful of songs I've made
my own to sing and play; clothes
and jewels that tell the world I am;
my dearest friends, who'll learn to do
the best they can without me;
poems not yet written; two daughters,
loved perhaps too much, who fill my life;
husband with his enfolding arms
and morning cups of tea:
this has to be faced up to.

But last to go and most lamented –
memories, held in the strongbox mind
to be taken out, relived –
how it felt to be there that one time
how the sun shone on the river, how
we laughed and cried and what was said.

The dead feel nothing, taste nothing.
No-one can touch them, they drift along
senselessly, floating like balloons, let go
into the stratosphere, mingling with stars,
aimless, surrounded by dead planets.

Biography

Angela Topping was born in 1954. After completing two English degrees at Liverpool University, marrying in 1976, she worked unhappily in the Civil Service, having steadfastly ignored all career advice because she wanted to be writer.

Her first collection was published in 1988 by *Stride*, three years after giving birth to her second daughter. The book led to involvement in education on several levels – poets in schools, evening class teaching and part time work in F.E. In 1992, she found herself teaching English full time in secondary school, moving schools after six years to her current post, on completion of her M.Ed. in Arts in Education.

A New and Selected poems, *The Fiddle*, was published in 1999. She also edited *The Least Thing*, an anthology of Christian Poetry, and *Making Connections*, a festschrift for Matt Simpson. Her own work continued to appear in anthologies such as *Frankenstein's Daughter*, *Poet's England* and *New Christian Poetry*.

Her interest in children's writing also flourished and her work is widely published in anthologies for children. She continues to promote a love of literature every day, and tells pupils that poetry is *chocolate for the mind*.